WORKBOOK FOR The ESL Writer's Handbook

2nd Edition

JANINE CARLOCK • MAEVE EBERHARDT

JAIME HORST • LIONEL MENASCHE

Pitt Series in English as a Second Language

ISBN-13: 978-0-472-03726-1

2021   2020   2019   2018   4   3   2   1

CONTENTS

SECTION 1

THE WRITING PROCESS

- Understanding Writing Assignments
- Generating Ideas

Understanding Writing Assignments
[*Handbook*, Section 1B, pages 7–10]

Exercise 1.1: Key Words in Writing Prompts

Match each key word with its definition. Write the letter of the definition next to the word in the space provided.

Group A

1. ____ *summarize*   a. give examples or an extended example
2. ____ *describe*   b. describe dissimilarities
3. ____ *narrate*   c. provide the main points only, with no details
4. ____ *illustrate*   d. provide general statements and details that present a clear idea
5. ____ *contrast*   e. explain the strong and weak points and give your opinion
6. ____ *evaluate*   f. tell the story of some events

Group B

1. ____ *challenge*   a. describe similarities and differences
2. ____ *assess*   b. present and discuss the weak points of an argument or explanation
3. ____ *prove*   c. describe the general class to which a thing belongs and how it differs
4. ____ *define*   from all others in that class
5. ____ *compare*   d. explain why something is true
6. ____ *review*   e. give a description of the issues involved
                        f. give a carefully thought-out judgment on something

Group C

1. ____ *outline*   a. explain the connections between two or more items
2. ____ *enumerate*   b. deal with, consider, discuss
3. ____ *address*   c. provide a description that focuses only on main ideas, with no details
4. ____ *relate*   d. describe a series of events in sequence
5. ____ *clarify*   e. give a descriptive list
6. ____ *trace*   f. explain in a way that makes the ideas easy to understand

Group D

1. ____ *explain*   a. present facts to show that an explanation is true
2. ____ *interpret*   b. provide information to make an issue clear
3. ____ *support*   c. explain the meaning
4. ____ *defend*   d. give arguments to support a position or claim against criticism
5. ____ *list*   e. provide a series of items

Group E

1. ____ *justify*   a. say what something is
2. ____ *discuss*   b. something done in steps or stages
3. ____ *state*   c. consider all aspects of an issue
4. ____ *criticize*   d. give reasons for doing or saying something
5. ____ *process*   e. evaluate the strong and weak points

Exercise 1.2: Identifying Key Words in Writing Assignments

Underline the key words in each writing assignment.

1. Discuss this proposition: All cultural and arts events and sites, such as libraries, concerts, museums, and festivals, should be made available to the public free or at little cost. Defend your position with facts and examples.

2. Describe the process of photosynthesis. Provide diagrams to support your explanation.

3. Trace the history of the roles of women and men in your country. Address economic and social aspects, and discuss changes that have occurred over the past century.

4. Compare two of the great revolutions in world history. Evaluate the reasons behind and the results of each revolution.

5. Assess the benefits and drawbacks of attending a university in a foreign country. Enumerate at least three issues that a student should or should not consider when choosing to study abroad, and support your opinion with examples and personal anecdotes.

Generating Ideas
[*Handbook,* Section 1D, pages 12–18]

. . . .
Exercise 1.3: Brainstorming

Imagine that you are going to write an essay on one of these topics. Brainstorm ideas for one of these topics. Use the space provided. Answers will vary.

1. travel

2. climate change

3. taking risks

Exercise 1.4: Discussion (Pair or Group Brainstorming)

With a partner or a small group, discuss one of these topics. Write some new ideas generated by your discussion in the space provided. Answers will vary.

1. Having practical experience is better than knowing theory.

2. National voluntary or military service should be required of all young people.

Exercise 1.5: Journalistic Questions

To help you generate more specific ideas for an essay, apply the journalistic questions (the *Wh-* words: *Who? When? Where? Why? What? How?*) to one of these topics. Write responses to each question in the space provided. Answers will vary.

1. internet addiction

2. English as a global language

Exercise 1.6: Freewriting (Writing without Stopping)

Choose one of these topics. Freewrite for three minutes in the space provided. Then underline some ideas from your freewriting that might be important to include in an essay on the chosen topic. Answers will vary.

1. being a vegan/vegetarian vs. eating meat

2. Learning never ends.

Exercise 1.7: Listing

Select one of these topics. Then list some ideas related to that topic in the space provided. Answers will vary.

1. being a vegan/vegetarian vs. eating meat

2. characteristics of a good leader

Exercise 1.8: Outlining

Choose one of these topics. Develop your ideas in an outline form by listing your main ideas and then adding more specific ideas under the main headings. Write your outline in the space provided. Answers will vary.

1. riding a bicycle safely

2. types of popular music

3. traditional holidays and festivals

4. choosing a field of study

5. the importance of studying history

6. electronic devices

Exercise 1.9: Visual Mapping (Clustering)

Choose one of these topics. Create a visual map to generate ideas about it. Diagram your map in the space provided. Answers will vary.

1. success

2. technology in education

3. politics

4. medicine

Exercise 1.10: Generating Ideas: Review

Choose one of the topics listed in *Workbook Exercise 1.2: Identifying Key Words in Writing Assignments* (page 3), and generate ideas about it as if you are planning to write an essay. Use one or more of the idea-generating techniques to develop your ideas: brainstorming, discussion, journalistic questions, freewriting, listing, outlining, or visual mapping. Write your ideas in the space provided. Answers will vary.

SECTION 2

ESSAY STRUCTURE

- Shaping a Paragraph
- Shaping an Essay

Shaping a Paragraph
[*Handbook*, Section 2A, pages 20–22]

Exercise 2.1: Topic and Comment

Circle the topic, and underline the perspective in each topic sentence.

1. My writing habits changed after taking the writing course.

2. There should not be mandatory curricula for young children.

3. Although both Shanghai and Hong Kong are cities in China, many cultural differences exist between them.

4. Parents should take responsibility for teaching their children how to behave and keep them quiet, especially in a public environment.

5. An excess of watching television can have harmful effects on children.

6. One of her favorite hobbies is knitting special items for her friends and family.

7. Growing vegetables in a home garden is a healthy and cost-effective source of food.

8. To maintain a healthy lifestyle, monitor your intake of sugar, salt, and fats.

Exercise 2.2: Finding a Topic Sentence in a Paragraph

Underline the topic sentence in the paragraph.

Paper, one of the most commonly used materials in daily life, is made from trees, a resource that can easily be exhausted on the earth. Generally, after using paper, people just throw it away. It takes 30 to 50 years to grow a tree, but the time we take to use paper and throw it away can be just a few minutes. We cannot grow trees as fast as we exhaust them. As a result, too many of the world's trees will be destroyed unless we find good ways to deal with the used paper. Trees also reduce the content of carbon dioxide in the air and improve the environment. Therefore, we should recycle used paper products as much as we can in order to save trees for other uses and have a better environment as well.

Exercise 2.3: Writing Topic Sentences

Write a possible topic sentence for each paragraph. Answers may vary.

1. Physical Activities make a better life for us. Sports make people an healthy and collaborative

First of all, sports can make people healthy, compared to playing computer games, playing cards, and so on. When you do fitness exercises, you can strengthen your body. When you swim, you can improve your flexibility. In addition, sports can make people more cooperative. For instance, in a soccer team, eleven people play together. The teammates need to cooperate with each other in order to win the match. If someone just wants to show off, the rate of success of the team will decrease.

2. Debit or credit cards?

When you are using a credit card, you are borrowing money from the credit card company. You can repay it when you want, but you also have to pay the interest. However, when you are using a debit card, you are using the money that is actually in your account. You are not allowed to overdraw, which means that you are not borrowing any money, and you do not need to pay any interest. Through a comparison, we find that debit cards have the benefits of credit cards, like convenience and safety, without the disadvantages of credit cards, namely, debt. In short, I suggest that the use of credit cards should be discouraged, and debit cards should be encouraged.

3. Culture build us Personality

Every community has its own cultural values that influence the lives and thoughts of the individuals living in that community. As part of my own community, I was influenced by certain social principles that contributed to shaping my life and choosing a specific major in my studies, disability and communication disorders. In addition, from my early childhood, I was taught by my parents to respect older people and help them, especially those who suffer from any kind of disability that could hinder certain aspects of their lives.

Exercise 2.4: Writing a Topic Sentence for a Paragraph

Write a possible topic sentence for the paragraph from an essay written by a student. Where would you place it? Explain your answer. Write your sentence and explanation in the space provided.

My parents used to always point out that helping people is a humane goal that is easy to understand but hard to fulfill. They used to stress the fact that helping people purifies the spirit and gets it used to good deeds. Actually, I know of a very revealing event related to this philosophy. It occurred to a friend of mine. One day, that friend was heading to my home for a visit. On his way, he encountered an old lady who had lost her money because a robber stole her wallet. She needed to take a taxi, and she had no money with her. So she asked my friend for help. My friend also had no money with him. He brought her with him to my place, borrowed some money from me, and then handed it to the lady. Two days later, my friend came back to visit me again and told me a strange event which had happened to him. He said that on the day when he helped that lady, he went home. When he got there, his mother told him that, on her way back home, she had lost her wallet somewhere, but fortunately there was somebody who handed her money to get back home. The amount of money was exactly the same as what my friend had given to help the old lady!

Your sentence: _Good social actions_ _____

_____

Shaping an Essay
[*Handbook*, Section 2B, pages 22–52]

Exercise 2.5: Essay Introduction

Read this introductory paragraph of an essay written by a student. Then answer the questions in the space provided.

There has always been a strong argument about human nature. Some say we are born evil and others say we are born benevolent. It seems that this is an argument without a definite answer. However, I would say absolutely that human nature is gracious. I think such a view is very important in my life because it has encouraged me to do volunteer work and has led me to study education and pursue it as my career. Also, what is more important is that it has enabled me to live happily and optimistically.

1. What do you think is the main idea of the whole essay?

    Human Nature

2. What are the main supporting ideas that you expect will be discussed in the body of the essay? Philosophy arguments about or Nature from Philosophers.
    Voluntary work
    Find a career
    I live happily and optimistically.

3. In what order do you think the supporting ideas will be discussed?
    — Human are born evil
                    benevolent
                    gracious

Exercise 2.6: Essay Conclusion

Read the concluding paragraph in an essay written by a student. Then answer the questions in the space provided.

> To sum up, I cannot deny that giving college credits is a way to encourage students to be volunteers, and some might be inspired during their work. However, we should realize that there are great differences between the whole-hearted type and the half-hearted type discussed. The former enjoy their volunteer work, and it could have a good effect on them. On the other hand, the latter tend to be impatient and feel annoyed easily. The work could have a bad effect on them, and they may do the work badly. Thus, even if our society encourages students to work as volunteers for college credits, it will not cause them all to become more gracious and helpful in the long run because volunteer work is not something easy that needs only one's time. Instead, it is a job that needs one's heart.

1. Based on this concluding paragraph, what do you think is the main idea of the whole essay? *Voluntary work for students to take credits to encourage.*

2. Based on this concluding paragraph, what are the main supporting ideas that you expect were discussed in the body of the essay? *Whole-hearted and half-hearted*

3. In what order do you think the supporting ideas were discussed? *whole hearted then half hearted*

Exercise 2.7: Essay Introduction and Conclusion

1. Underline the thesis statement of the essay in the introductory paragraph.
2. Note the map (or foreshadowing) in the paragraph, and list what you expect the main points of the essay will be.
3. Underline the restatement of the thesis in the concluding paragraph.

Introduction

A friend for me is a person whom I can trust and whom I can count on in different places and in different moments. Since about 1980, I can identify three distinct periods in my life in terms of my social environment and friendships. The first period started at the beginning of my elementary school and ended when I finished high school; the second started with my undergraduate studies and ended with my Master thesis; the last one began with my PhD studies in August 2002 and continues up to now. During all these periods of my life, I met different kinds of people and I made a lot of friends who were quite important to me.

Conclusion

What I can conclude from this is that during all the time I have been a student, I have made many friends who have been a significant part of my life. I am convinced that nobody can live without friends. Certainly, if I hadn't made all these friends I would be a very different person today. In each stage of life, it is important to have people you can count on and who will help you on your journey through new challenges and experiences.

2. Main points expected:

_____

_____

_____

_____

Exercise 2.8: Description

Using descriptive language, write a brief paragraph (three to five sentences) on one of these topics. Answers will vary. Write your paragraph in the space provided.

1. a teacher or role model that you remember from your childhood

2. a favorite song, musical composition, play, or movie

3. a beautiful or memorable place that you have visited

4. the process of making your favorite meal or dish

5. something you did that was challenging but that you succeeded in doing

6. a book that made a lasting impression on you

Exercise 2.9: Simple Definition

Write a simple definition for each word. Answers will vary.

1. bus _____

_____

2. mouse _____

_____

3. cheese _____

_____

4. calendar _____

_____

5. sunscreen _____

_____

6. headphones _____

_____

7. elevator _____

_____

8. umbrella _____

_____

Exercise 2.10: Complex Definition

Write a complex definition (one brief paragraph) for each word. Answers will vary. Write your definitions in the space provided.

1. language

2. home

3. rice

4. friendship

5. online translators

Exercise 2.11: Examples

Find the sentence in the paragraph that needs an example or detail as support. Create a logical example, and place it in the paragraph after that sentence. Write your example in the space provided, and use arrows to show where in the paragraph you would place it.

Pacer Construction Company has demonstrated strong performance on past projects and has built a good reputation among its clients. Pacer has finished all of its projects with good quality and on schedule, while often ending up under budget. That is why a large number of its clients are highly satisfied with Pacer's performance and the company has received numerous awards for its work. This recognition for its work directly reflects Pacer's work performance and the good reputation that it has built over four decades of construction experience.

Exercise 2.12: Paragraph Unity

This paragraph lacks unity because some sentences are not related to the topic. Make the paragraph more unified by removing the sentences or phrases that are not related to the main idea of the paragraph. Write the numbers of the deleted sentences in the space provided. [Sentences are numbered only for reference in this exercise.]

①️ Diabetes can be divided into two categories. ②️ One is Insulin-Dependent Diabetes (IDDs, Type I diabetes) and the other is Non–Insulin Dependent Diabetes (NIDDs, Type II diabetes). ③️ It is likely that everyone knows someone who has diabetes. ④️ Both types of diabetes greatly increase a person's risk for a range of serious conditions such as blindness and kidney failure. ⑤️ Thus it is important to have a good relationship with one's doctor. ⑥️ Older people tend to have a wide range of health issues, including breathing difficulties, heart conditions, and circulatory problems. ⑦️ Moreover, diabetics can have critical risk factors for heart disease, stroke, and leg amputations. ⑧️ Although both types of diabetes are related with excess glucose concentration in blood, each has its own distinguished characteristics in causes, symptoms, and treatments. ⑨️ Maintaining one's health can be quite expensive, especially when one must deal with serious health problems such as diabetes.

Sentences deleted to improve unity (write the sentence numbers):

Exercise 2.13: Creating Paragraph Coherence

The sentences of this paragraph, written by a student, have been moved out of their original order. Rearrange the order of sentences to create a coherent paragraph. Write the new coherent paragraph in the space provided. More than one order is possible. [Sentences are numbered only for reference in this exercise.]

① Overall, the wine and champagne industries are very significant to the economic health of my hometown. ② Once a year the people in the rural areas harvest those grapes and sell them to companies that make several kinds of wine, juice, and champagne. ③ Grapes are the main product that is cultivated in our region. ④ For people who like to know about wine and champagne there are several places where they can learn about the origin of the wine industry, see some of the local products, and taste some of the special wines and champagnes. ⑤ My hometown is a small, quiet city, and its economy is based on agriculture and tourism. ⑥ Additionally, tourism also makes its contribution to the regional economy.

Order of sentences to improve coherence (write the sentence numbers):

Exercise 2.14: Paragraph Coherence

These paragraphs lack coherence. Rewrite the paragraphs so that they are more coherent. Use transitions, repeated key words, synonyms, and reference words to improve coherence. Answers may vary.

1. My own experiences and my observations of others support the generalization that one must seek a deeper reason for the anger within oneself rather than looking to the outside. It is true that anger can be generated from relationships with others, but it is we ourselves who feel it. When we are frustrated by something, the degrees of anger vary according to our character, situation, place, and, scientifically, our genetic orientation. We have the experience of reacting differently to the same situation depending on our mood. We cannot rely on the external factors to change so that we can avoid anger because anger is an internal reaction to what is happening around us. Anger and the situations that cause anger are unavoidable, but we can train ourselves to deal with anger so that anger does not overcome us and affect other people in negative ways.

2. My family recently traveled to South America. We went to South America to have a vacation. We live in the United States. The United States is in the northern hemisphere. We visited Argentina. Argentina is in the southern hemisphere. It was July when we traveled. When we left home we were wearing t-shirts and sandals. When we got to Argentina we needed to put on coats and shoes with socks. In the southern hemisphere it is winter in July, and in the northern hemisphere it is summer in July. During our vacation it was sunny and it was not as cold as it is in winter where we live. We stayed for one month. It was funny that we needed such different clothing after just one plane ride.

Exercise 2.15: Using Transitions for Coherence in a Paragraph

Choose an appropriate transition word or phrase to fill each blank in the paragraph. Think about the logical connection that needs to be made between the ideas. Answers may vary.

The internet affects our lives in many ways today. ① _____, we can communicate with each other by email easily, compared to sending messages by postal mail. ② _____, we can chat with our friends, no matter where they are. ③ _____, we can buy whatever we want on the internet, and we do not need to go out to the shops. ④ _____, we can pay our bills such as electric fee and gas fee, and manage our accounts online. ⑤ _____, the internet has some disadvantages for people. There is too much information on the internet that is not very useful for us, and some information from the internet is not accurate at all. ⑥ _____, the internet reduces the interaction of people to some extent. ⑦ _____, your friend may just send an email to you instead of visiting you in person. That will decrease the opportunities for you to meet each other face to face. ⑧ _____, people can just chat at home on the internet rather than going out with their friends. ⑨ _____, while the internet may make our lives more convenient in many ways, the internet also decreases our social interaction and makes our lives more isolated.

Exercise 2.16: Using Transitions for Coherence in an Essay

The transitions have been deleted in this essay. Provide an appropriate transition for each blank space to create coherence. Answers may vary.

Employment and Taxes

① _____, many developing countries face economic problems resulting from different factors. Some people claim that the problems are too difficult to solve. There are, ② _____, positive ways to improve the economic situation of countries and promote the lives of their poor people. These must include an increase in job opportunities and a decrease in the amount of taxes. Increasing employment and decreasing taxes will improve the economic situation of a country and reduce the rate of poverty.

③ _____ , employment is the active engine that keeps a country going. It is the means by which people are able to care for themselves and their families. ④ _____, job opportunities maintain a certain economic security for people and enable them to improve their lives. This means that they can care for their families and be active, contributing citizens. ⑤ _____ , jobs are a symbol of independence and self-sufficiency. A person who is self-sufficient does not need the help of governmental social programs like welfare or medical insurance for assistance in his or her life. ⑥ _____, this individual's self-sufficiency would save money for the government.

⑦ _____, unemployment is the negative condition that keeps an economy in an unfavorable and inactive state. Lack of employment is a serious problem for the individual in the sense that he or she will be and will feel dependent and lost. ⑧ _____, he or she may depend on the government to provide the basic needs for him or her. The government, ⑨ _____, loses resources and money in supporting such a person.

⑩ _____, another economic aspect that negatively affects a government is high taxes. Most people complain too much about the large amount of taxes they have to pay to the government. They claim that they cannot afford necessities because they find themselves left with little money. They cannot save money for later situations of need because the amount of their taxes is far out of proportion to their income. Taxes which are too great and which put a person in a tight situation badly affect the population and the economy. ⑪ _____, some economists assert that there should be low, fair, and balanced tax regulations that take into consideration people's personal financial situations and create opportunities for them to live a better life. ⑫ _____, despite economists' strong support of low taxes, it must be emphasized that they do not want taxes to be eliminated altogether. They realize governments must have revenues to use in social services and job creation. Before setting tax levels, governments should provide jobs to enhance people's economic situation. ⑬ _____, there should be a fair decision about the amount of taxes to be paid, taking into account the cost of living and the person's ability to pay a certain amount.

⑭ _____ , high rates of unemployment and high taxes cause economic problems and lead governments into many financial crises. It is only by giving serious consideration to people's financial situations and providing them with jobs that an economy can be improved and stimulated.

SECTION 3

PATTERNS OF ORGANIZATION

3

- Narrative Essay
- Process Essay
- Comparison/Contrast Essay
- Cause-and-Effect Essay
- Argument Essay

Narrative Essay
[*Handbook*, Section 3A, pages 62–68]

. . . .
Exercise 3.1: Ordering a Narrative Paragraph

Put the sentences in narrative order by numbering them 1–13. The first one has been done for you as an example.

_____ a. Meanwhile, the campers were talking about how much fun the night was going to be.

_____ b. I don't know what the others wished for, but I wished that I would again have as much fun at the next year's camp.

_____ c. This was upsetting because we all wanted to have a last chance to all be together and have fun.

_____ d. That was when we found out that it was one of the best nights for seeing meteor showers.

__1__ e. One of my best memories took place when I was working at a children's summer camp last year.

_____ f. On Thursday, the counselors and campers had planned a big bonfire and then, later, a star-gazing session, but it had rained heavily.

_____ g. After dinner, we all gathered in a big clearing by the lake and lit the bonfire we had prepared.

_____ h. It was the last weekend for many of the children at camp and everyone was feeling a bit sad.

_____ i. For hours, we all watched shooting stars together.

_____ j. All day, the counselors searched for dry wood and set it up for the bonfire.

_____ k. As the bonfire died down, we all brought out our blankets and lay down to look at the stars.

_____ l. So the next night, everyone was even more eager to have end-of-the-summer fun.

_____ m. We sang songs and roasted marshmallows.

Exercise 3.2: Practice with *When* and *While*

Connect the sentences using *when*, *while*, or *whenever*. If more than one can be used, write both answers on the line provided.

1. _____ he was a junior in college, he met his future wife.

2. We were just leaving the baseball field _____ a tornado struck.

3. _____ I was watching TV, my brother came home from football practice.

4. _____ they learned that their daughter had been in an accident, they immediately rushed to the hospital.

5. _____ I was young, I used to spend a lot of time at my grandparents. I have fond memories of Sunday mornings spent reading the comics section with my grandfather _____ my grandmother baked homemade bread. To this day, _____ I smell freshly baked bread, I think of those happy times.

6. I had asked my neighbor many times not to play loud music in the afternoon _____ my baby was sleeping, but he would not stop. _____ I just couldn't take it anymore, I finally had to complain to the building manager.

7. At camp, since I didn't like to swim, I would help prepare lunch _____ the other campers were enjoying swimming in the lake.

8. Do you remember a day _____ you were so happy you wished that day could last forever?

Process Essay
[*Handbook,* Section 3B, pages 68–72]

. . . .

Exercise 3.3: Practice with Process Words and Phrases

Underline the process words or phrases in the paragraph. The first one has been done for you as an example.

How to Find a Doctor

Choosing a physician who will oversee your health care can be a difficult decision, but the process can be made less stressful by following a few simple steps. It is important to work through this process before you urgently need health care, so that you can make a wise and carefully thought-out decision. <u>An initial step</u> in this process is to ask friends for recommendations. Although your experience with a particular doctor may differ from another person's, these opinions can be very valuable in helping you to narrow your search to just a few doctors. Once you have a list of several doctors for whom you have received personal recommendations, you should call each office to ask a few questions: Is the practice accepting new patients? Can the doctor address your (or your family's) particular health concerns? You should also note whether the staff seem professional and friendly. Another very important step in this process is to find out whether your insurance company will cover visits to the physician that you select. You should check with both your insurance company and the doctor's office to verify this. If the answers to your initial questions are positive, a subsequent but optional step is to visit the office in person. Besides determining the convenience of the location, you can observe the atmosphere of the waiting room and examination rooms, and the personalities and mannerisms of the office staff and nurses. A visit also gives you the opportunity to interview the physician and ascertain his or her personality and approach to health care. To complete the process of selecting a doctor, you should inform both the doctor's office and your insurance company of your decision, so that there are no delays or complications when the time comes for you and your family to rely on your doctor's expertise.

Exercise 3.4: Connecting Ideas Using Process Words and Phrases

Connect and/or change the sentences to create a process paragraph. Not every sentence will need to be changed. Some sentences may need to be combined. Answers will vary. Write your paragraph in the space provided.

How to Choose a Major

In choosing a major you should . . .

1. Talk with an advisor at your college or university.

2. Ask your friends if they know any good advisors at your college or university. Try to choose an advisor with interests similar to yours so you can be sure that he or she will have valuable information to share.

3. Tell the advisor about yourself.

4. Let the advisor know what you think your interests are.

5. He or she will give you advice about which departments might be the best for you.

6. Go to the department(s) that your advisor recommended and get more information.

7. Be sure to carefully consider the information you have collected.

8. Discuss the information and your options with friends and family.

9. Consider their advice and your own inclination.

10. Make an informed decision.

Comparison/Contrast Essay
[*Handbook*, Section 3C, pages 72–80]

Exercise 3.5: Connecting Ideas Using Comparison/Contrast Words and Phrases

Connect the pairs of phrases using comparison/contrast vocabulary. Try not to use the same connecting word(s) more than once. Write one comparison and one contrast sentence. Answers will vary.

<u>Example</u>

big cities / small towns

a. **Both** *big cities* **and** *small towns must offer public education for their children.* [comparison]

b. **However,** *in big cities, schools are usually overcrowded,* **while** *in small towns, classes are small.* [contrast]

1. *online shopping / shopping in a store*

   a.

   b.

2. *older people / younger people*

   a.

   b.

3. *fast food restaurant / sit-down restaurant*

   a.

   b.

4. *eating with a fork / eating with chopsticks*

   a.

   b.

5. *tropical climate / temperate climate*

   a.

   b.

Exercise 3.6: Using Comparison/Contrast Words to Create a Paragraph

Using comparison/contrast vocabulary, create an effective paragraph based on the framework of information given. Use the chart to take notes. Add any additional points. Answers will vary. Write your paragraph in the space provided.

A. Cell Phone Plans in the U.S.	**B.** Cell Phone Plans in Another Country
Cost of phone:	Cost of phone:
Available accessories:	Available accessories:
Price per minute:	Price per minute:
Prices at different times of the day and night/weekend:	Prices at different times of the day and night/weekend:
Different plans:	Different plans:
Ability to call internationally:	Ability to call internationally:
Additional points:	Additional points:

Cause-and-Effect Essay
[*Handbook,* Section 3D, pages 81–85]

Exercise 3.7: Identifying Cause-and-Effect Words and Phrases

Underline the cause-and-effect words and phrases.

The Changing of the World with the Advent of the Internet

Imagine a situation where the current internet system does not work any more. You can see long lines of people who are waiting to pay bills at banks. At the beginning of the semester, college offices are filled with students who want to register for their classes. Unemployment is up as many people working at companies based on the internet are out of work. Clearly, even though only a few decades have passed since the internet started to become commonly used, we can realize that the internet has greatly affected many parts of our lives.

First of all, the most important effect of the internet has been to increase accessibility of information. The internet allows people to get information easily, no matter the place or time. People do not need to go to the library and read several books to get information. That is because Google, the most popular web search engine, can show the web pages containing information people are searching within just a few seconds. Likewise, conventional encyclopedias in the library are not used so much any more because most people use Wikipedia, one of the biggest information providers on the internet. Thus, most students, researchers, and even common people would be very inconvenienced if the internet were no longer available. This demonstrates the important position the internet holds in our daily lives.

Moreover, the internet has played a great role in facilitating interpersonal communication. For supporting examples one need look no further than email. Today, most students and workers turn on their computer in the morning and check email first. To send and receive email takes less than one minute. Many international students also use Skype, the internet messenger program, to talk with their family. This program does not involve high cost or much time compared to phone calls or letters. As a consequence, people feel free to contact even those who are very far away using the internet. This definitely has a positive impact on foreign students, who are far from home and may be feeling lonely due to culture shock. The fact that these students can easily communicate with their friends and family abroad leads to a sense of community and well-being that may help them through their period of culture shock.

Moreover, online shopping has become quite popular as a result of the now common use of the internet. In my observation, most people know the first step to buy products at a cheaper price is to search at sites such as Amazon. In fact, today, there are lots of online shopping malls that sell products at reasonable prices compared to regular malls because online shopping mall owners do not need to pay for rent. Also, customers do not need to drive to the mall, so they can save time as well as money. This is another way in which the internet has greatly affected our lives.

Finally, the most striking effect of the internet has been the advent of online services. Today, people use many kinds of online services. People often pay bills using online banking. Students tend to register for classes or hand in their homework online. Many governments provide online services including registration for the driver's test and photo ID to shorten citizens' waiting time at the office. Because it is so simple, using online services has become part of our daily lives as well, and the internet is the phenomenon that has made it possible.

The internet has greatly affected our lives. It helps us access information easily any place or time. We can communicate with those who live very far away using email and some internet-based programs at less cost and in less time. Furthermore, not only online shopping but also online services make it possible to decrease our effort to go to the store, bank, and government offices. Our lives have gradually changed due to the internet so that now we might even say it has become a necessity.

Exercise 3.8: Connecting Ideas Using Cause-and-Effect Words and Phrases

Use words or phrases to connect cause-and-effect ideas in the paragraph by filling the blanks. The first one has been done for you as an example. Answers may vary. [Sentences are numbered only for reference in this exercise.]

In the U.S. the divorce rate continues to rise every year. ① <u>One reason for</u> this constant increase is the fact that divorces have become so common. Before the 1980s, divorced people were not viewed as the norm. The commonly accepted belief was that these people should have tried harder to work out their marital difficulties. Now, however, ② _____ such a high percentage of married people get divorced, it may seem like a normal part of life. With more than 50% of marriages in the U.S. eventually ending in divorce, no one can take the attitude that divorced people are "strange." In addition, ③ _____ there is no longer a social taboo against getting a divorce, people do not feel compelled to "stick it out." ④ _____ a situation in which couples may go into a marriage thinking, "If it doesn't work out, I can always get a divorce." A typical ⑤ _____ of this kind of thinking is that when a difficult problem arises, rather than working hard to solve it or accepting that a compromise might be the only way to solve the problem, the couple uses divorce as a solution.

Argument Essay
[*Handbook,* Section 3E, pages 86–94]

. . . .
Exercise 3.9: Identifying Argument Words and Phrases

Underline the argument words and phrases used in the text. Remember that cause-and-effect expressions can also contribute to the development of an argument.

Early Computer Education:
Its Negative Effects on the Intellectual Development of Children

Imagine a group of kindergarten students sitting in front of their screens in the computer room of an elementary school. They look into the dazzling images on their individually assigned computer screen while hardly talking to each other. No smile or liveliness can be found in this room, where these 6-year-old children start learning how to adapt themselves to the so-called age of information technology. Even though the computer is now an essential part of modern life, it doesn't seem logical to waste valuable childhood years when children should be performing creative activities and discovering life for themselves. In fact, this type of computer education in early elementary years has several negative effects on the intellectual development of children: lowering their concentration on a task, preventing them from acquiring social skills, and exposing them to a hazardous online environment.

First of all, early computer education can lower children's concentration on a task. While young children learn on the computer, they use lots of software or computer games which contain attractive images. Even though they seem to pay attention to the work on the computer, actually they are just looking at the monitor, overwhelmed by the glittering pictures. This strong visual stimulation irritates children's minds and the children are apt to lose interest in things without such a dazzling display. It seems for them so boring and dumb to read a storybook because it is not moving fast or shining with bright images. As a result, children can be easily distracted and cannot concentrate on the important tasks for their ages such as reading books, writing their opinions, or solving logical problems, which are definitely needed for their academic success and mental growth. We can deduce that this will lead to problems for the children later in life when these skills are necessary.

Another negative effect of early computer education is that children lose time and opportunity to socialize with peers. Because most children tend to work on the computer alone for a long time, they confine themselves in virtual space and are reluctant to interact with peers. Even though they need lots of social experiences in early childhood to grow into a well-rounded person, children can be easily involved in computer activity and may spend all of their free time doing something on the computer. Consequently, they are deprived of important opportunities to play and talk with their friends. It is reasonable to assume, then, that in this type of situation, where children grow up into adults without sufficient opportunity to interact with peers, they may have less of a capability to participate in our complex and interactive society.

Finally, children can be exposed to the hazardous online environment. For example, there is a great deal of inappropriate material on the internet like pornography, violence, and hatred. Those things exert a very bad influence on children. Because children are so sensitive and do not have much knowledge of life, they accept the dangerous influences as reality. In addition, they can encounter bullies or molesters via chatting or email. Due to the anonymity, a criminal can easily approach the innocent children and lure them into a very harmful situation. Therefore, children may experience physical danger as well.

In conclusion, early computer education may have a negative impact on children with respect to the development of concentration and social skills and to the possibility of harmful internet experiences. Therefore, it is better to teach children how to use a computer in their later elementary grades, taking into consideration their developmental stages. In doing this, we will be able to minimize the negative effects of children's computer education.

Exercise 3.10: Connecting Ideas Using Logical Argument

Insert one or two sentences that logically connect Statements A and C in each of the groups of argument sentences. Answers will vary.

Example

    A. Most college students have many things to do in addition to their schoolwork.

    B. For example, many students have part-time jobs and participate in extra-curricular activities such as sports and clubs. These activities may be time-consuming and can detract from the time students spend on studying.

    C. Consequently, having tests helps students stay focused on their schoolwork.

Argument 1

    A. The amount of violence on television seems to be steadily increasing.

    B.

    C. Parents must therefore pay close attention to what their children watch on television.

Argument 2

    A. Antioxidants such as beta-carotene and lycopene are found in many fruits and vegetables.

    B.

    C. Thus, diets rich in fruits and vegetables may help reduce the risk of cancer.

Exercise 3.11: Making Generalizations

Write a generalization that can be made for each group of sentences. Answers may vary.

1. Heesung, Maria, and Abdullah are all students in an engineering class. Heesung has recently won an award for her research. Maria has a scholarship to study at the university for two years. Abdullah has been elected president of the Student Engineering Organization.

   The students in the engineering class _____

   _____

2. Akiko Yokohama has studied French for nine years. Her brother, Taro, works as a translator for a financial company in Germany. Their mother teaches English at a school in Tokyo.

   *Members of the Yokohama family*_____

   _____

3. In Hunter's Woods, 25 murders took place last year. There were also 53 cases of robbery and 10 drive-by shootings.

   The city of Hunter's Woods _____

   _____

4. Colleges are using online systems for grading. They are also using online systems for posting syllabi and providing online bulletin boards for students to post on.

   Colleges _____

   _____

5. Parents use lullabies to help put their babies to sleep. Many hospitals use music therapy to help their patients feel better. Many people, after coming home from a long day at work, put some music on to help them relax.

   Music _____

   _____

SECTION 4

RESEARCH PAPER

- Finding Sources
- Summarizing, Paraphrasing, and Using Quotations
- Outlining
- Writing Thesis Statements
- APA Style References
- MLA Style Works Cited

4

Finding Sources [*Handbook*, Section 4B, pages 105–109]

. . . .

Exercise 4.1: Evaluating Sources

Imagine that you are writing a paper on the benefits of using technology in the classroom. Use Google, Google Scholar, and/or your library's online research databases to find the source type listed. Provide brief notes for each of the criteria listed. Then answer whether you would use it in a research paper and explain your answer.

1. An online journal

Title of journal: _____

Title of article: _____

Author: _____

Source: _____

Relevance: _____

_____

Accuracy of information: _____

_____

Purpose: _____

_____

Currency: _____

Use this source?   Yes / No / Maybe

Why or why not? _____

_____

2. A website

URL and title of website (or part of website): _____

_____

Author: _____

Source: _____

Relevance: _____

_____

Accuracy of information: _____

_____

Purpose: _____

_____

Currency: _____

Use this source?   Yes / No / Maybe

Why or why not? _____

_____

3. An online news article

Title of newspaper: _____

Title of article: _____

Author: _____

Source: _____

Relevance: _____

Accuracy of information: _____

_____

Purpose: _____

_____

Currency: _____

Use this source?   Yes / No / Maybe

Why or why not? _____

_____

Summarizing, Paraphrasing, and Using Quotations [*Handbook*, Section 4D, pages 112–119]

. . . .

Exercise 4.2: Summarizing

Write a paraphrased summary of each passage from a student research paper in two or three sentences in the space provided. (A paraphrased summary uses your own words or phrases, your own sentence structure, and your own order of information.) Try underlining important ideas, circling key words and phrases, and taking some brief notes.

Passage A

Smoking has become a big issue and a very common habit. Some people start with this habit because of stress, and others because they think it is "trendy." Despite the warnings given by doctors about negative side-effects of smoking, people continue to smoke and tend to not care a lot about it. Why is this serious problem underestimated by smokers? Is smoking really that dangerous? The truth is that tobacco contains many dangerous substances, including nicotine, which is a highly addictive drug that makes it difficult for smokers to quit. As we know nicotine is a dangerous and addictive substance, but cigarettes also have more than 4,000 chemical substances that are harmful for human health including benzene, arsenic, butane, DDT, toluene, and vinyl chloride (Healthy Living Now). Sixty-nine of these chemical substances are known carcinogens, meaning that they are known to cause cancer.

Furthermore, smoking for a long period (meaning 10 years or more), has progressive ill effects on the respiratory system. Lung disease is a common and serious illness in smokers who have smoked for at least a decade. The American Lung Association explains that some health problems develop very gradually, but after 10 years of tobacco use people's lungs are seriously damaged and smokers are in danger of death from emphysema. Smoking is responsible for 90% of all lung disease and 75% of chronic bronchitis. Clearly, smoking is a serious threat to people's health.

_____

_____

_____

_____

Passage B

Some may say that college is a place for nurturing and learning, and thus studying in college is not a big deal. However, many students spend a great deal of their time, mental focus, and physical energy on studying and feel a lot of pressure to get high grades. Even those students who really love their majors and classes still need to put plenty of effort into their studies, which can bring on psychological stress and affect their physical health. College students work hard for many reasons—to have a high grade point average (GPA), to gain internships or research opportunities, and even to achieve successful jobs. To achieve all of this, students often trade their cheerfulness, sleep, social time, and hobbies to their GPAs. In a word, they are inevitably influenced by the expectation of high grades and trade their "life" to GPAs, placing their GPA over anything else.

Students who focus excessively on their grades, however, will find that many other parts of their lives are suffering. They may lose friends as they spend all of their free time with their books and computer rather than building relationships. They may fall ill or feel depressed if they do not allow themselves a healthy amount of time to eat, sleep, and exercise. And they might miss out on some of the exciting experiences that college offers—experiences that are unique to their years in college and that they will never be able to recreate after their college years are over. Students must realize that grades are not the most important thing in life—finding your life's passion and creating your own life values are a key part of your college education. For example, a student who values novelty, practicality, and creativity in life may choose engaging in a start-up technology company as a specific goal. High grades may not be the first priority of that student, but she will feel fulfilled and excited about her life's work. This is the best way to get the most out of college, rather than focusing only on having a perfect GPA.

_____

_____

_____

_____

Passage C

Fluctuations in global temperatures and climate patterns have been occurring for thousands of years, but global warming—a type of climate change that involves an increase in the Earth's average temperature—is becoming an increasingly serious threat for people nowadays. Earth's population is increasing and so people are consuming more energy than in the past, causing increased levels of carbon dioxide in the atmosphere, which results in warmer temperatures on earth due to the "greenhouse effect." Some scientists warn of the possible threats to life on the planet as a result of global warming.

One possible effect of climate change could be the melting of ice in the Arctic and Antarctic regions. Some research has found that climate change has already had a negative impact on people's lives in the Arctic, in terms of the population of animals on which they rely for food. Melting polar ice will also lead to the rising of sea levels, which would lead to flooding that would destroy houses, farms, and the whole way of life for millions of people in coastal areas all around the world. There may also be a negative impact on people's health due to global warming. Some scientists predict that increases in global temperatures could cause faster reproduction of mosquitoes and a broader area where they can thrive, since they rely on warm temperatures to reproduce. Greater numbers of mosquitoes would likely result in higher rates of serious mosquito-borne diseases such as Zika virus, yellow fever, and malaria.

_____

_____

_____

_____

_____

_____

_____

Exercise 4.3: Recognizing Plagiarism

Each original sentence is shown together with the way it was used in a research paper. Decide whether or not the use is plagiarism. Explain your decision by writing the letter of the appropriate reason: A, B, C, D, or E.

Reasons:

A. Not plagiarism: Original words quoted with quotation marks and with citation.

B. Not plagiarism: Complete paraphrase with citation.

C. Plagiarism: Original words quoted but with no quotation marks.

D. Plagiarism: Some paraphrase but sentence structure is the same and some original words are quoted with no quotation marks.

E. Plagiarism: Quotation or paraphrase is correct but the citation is missing.

> **Source of Numbers 1–3**: Unger, E. (2017, May 3). These salt flats are one of the most remarkable vistas on earth. *National Geographic*. Retrieved from http://www.nationalgeographic.com/travel/destinations/south-america/bolivia/how-to-see-salar-de-uyuni-salt-flats-bolivia/

1. **Original:** Stretching more than 4,050 square miles of the Altiplano, Bolivia's Salar de Uyuni is the world's largest salt flat, left behind by prehistoric lakes evaporated long ago.

   Use: The largest salt flat in the world, the Salar de Uyuni in Bolivia, was formed by now-evaporated prehistoric lakes and is over 4,050 square miles in area (Unger, 2017).

   _____

2. **Original:** Here, a thick crust of salt extends to the horizon, covered by quilted, polygonal patterns of salt rising from the ground.

   Use: A thick crust of salt goes all the way to the horizon, covered by polygonal patterns of salt that rise from the ground (Unger, 2017).

   _____

3. **Original:** This beautiful and otherworldly terrain serves as a lucrative extraction site for salt and lithium—the element responsible for powering laptops, smart phones, and electric cars.

   Use: This "beautiful and otherworldly terrain" is also a source of both salt and lithium, which is used in a wide variety of electronics, from cell phones to electric cars (Unger, 2017).

   _____

Source of Numbers 4–8: Panko, B. (2017, July 20). Humans have produced nine billion tons of plastic and counting. *Smithsonian.com*. Retrieved from http://www.smithsonianmag.com/smart-news/humans-are-burying-earth-under-billions-tons-plastic-180964125/

4. **Original:** New research shows that humans have produced just over 9 billion tons of plastic since 1950, with much of it still sitting around in our landfills and oceans.

   Use: Recent research shows that since 1950 people have produced over 9 billion tons of plastic, and much of this plastic remains in landfills and oceans (Panko, 2017).

   _____

5. **Original:** Previous research has found that there may be more than 250,000 tons of plastic currently floating in Earth's oceans, much of it in the form of tiny chunks that can easily be carried by currents and consumed by sea creatures big and small.

   Use: The more than 250,000 tons of plastic dispersed throughout the oceans poses a great risk to a variety of sea creatures, both large and small, which may swallow the small pieces of plastic (Panko, 2017).

   _____

6. **Original:** Some scientists have proposed using organisms to degrade the plastics, which left on its own rarely degrades in nature.

   Use: Since plastic does not naturally deteriorate on its own, scientists are examining ways to use organisms to break down the material (Panko, 2017).

   _____

7. **Original:** The only permanent way to get rid of our plastic products is incineration, but only about 12 percent of plastic has ever met this fate. And researchers disagree about the safety of burning plastic, which has the potential to release a host of toxic chemicals into the environment.

   Use: Although burning is a good way to dispose of plastic permanently, it is very rarely done and, when it is done, can release toxins into the air.

   _____

8. **Original:** The most effective solution, however, may be changing our reliance on plastic.

   Use: The best solution to the plastic problem may be to change our reliance on plastic.

   _____

Source of Numbers 9–13: Kitchakarn, O. (2016). How students perceived social media as a learning tool in enhancing their language learning performance. *TOJET: The Turkish Online Journal of Educational Technology, 15,* 53–60. Retrieved from https://eric.ed.gov/?id=EJ1117631

9. **Original:** Technology is currently being used to make teaching and learning more engaging and stimulating.

   Use: Technology is currently being used to make teaching and learning more engaging and stimulating.

   _____

10. **Original:** Apparently, Facebook is highly likely to prove advantageous to students should it be capitalized on as part of the learning process.

    Use: Kitchakarn (2016) asserts that "Facebook is highly likely to prove advantageous to students should it be capitalized on as part of the learning process" (p. 53).

    _____

11. **Original:** Even though this research revealed that students viewed Facebook favorably as an online learning tool, more studies should be conducted to find out whether and to what extent Facebook can help improve students' English competency in the long run.

    Use: One study demonstrates that students have favorable opinions regarding Facebook as a tool in their language learning; however, in order to examine how useful Facebook can be in improving students' language skills over the long term, more research is needed.

    _____

12. **Original:** In addition, choosing the right type of social media has a huge impact on participation.

    Use: Participation is influenced strongly by the type of social media chosen (Kitchakarn, 2016, p. 60).

    _____

13. **Original:** Facebook can be a platform of supplementary materials that teachers provide for learners to study outside class in order to gain knowledge.

    Use: Facebook can serve as way to provide extra materials for students so that they can study outside class in order to gain knowledge.

    _____

Source of Numbers 14–16: Beeler, C. (2017, July 21). A super-simple strategy may be key to fighting climate change. *PRI's The World*. Retrieved from www.pri.org/stories/2017-07-21/super-simple-strategy-may-be-key-fighting-climate-change

14. **Original:** In recent years, developed countries have committed billions of dollars to help developing countries prevent deforestation.

    Use: According to Beeler (2017), "In recent years, developed countries have committed billions of dollars to help developing countries prevent deforestation."

    _____

15. **Original:** A new study is the first to analyze a landowner payment program in a randomized trial—the gold standard of field research that is common in many areas of study but rare in conservation.

    Use: A new study is the first to analyze a landowner payment program in a randomized trial—the gold standard of field research that is common in many areas of study but rare in conservation (Beeler, 2017).

    _____

16. **Original:** If the program became permanent, Jayachandran estimated the cost of averting a metric ton of carbon would be $2.60, significantly less than the so-called social cost of carbon, which the Environmental Protection Agency in 2012 assessed at roughly $39.

    Use: Researchers estimate that long-term use of this program would incur a cost of $2.60 per metric ton of carbon averted, a significant difference from the Environmental Protection Agency's 2012 estimate of a social cost of $39 per metric ton of carbon (Beeler, 2017).

    _____

Outlining
[*Handbook*, Section 4E, pages 120–121]

Exercise 4.4: Ordering Outline Headings

The headings and subheadings of the outline are listed in a jumbled order and with no indentation. Rearrange the list into an outline using the template to show the relative importance of ideas. Answers may vary.

Title: *The Benefits of Participating in a Study Group*

Get a support system

Several benefits to participating in a study group

Can practice new study skills in a group setting

Can contact someone in the group to get notes if you miss a class

Get new perspectives from discussion with other students

Helps you think more deeply about the topic you are studying

Can see how others study

Learn new study skills

Have someone to ask if you don't understand something in class

Understand the subject better

Main Idea: _____

1. _____

    a. _____

    b. _____

2. _____

    a. _____

    b. _____

3. _____

    a. _____

    b. _____

Writing Thesis Statements
[*Handbook*, Section 4F, pages 121–123]

Exercise 4.5: Thesis Statements: Argument or Report?

Examine each sentence. If the sentence is the main focus of a **report paper**, circle **R**. If it is the main focus of an **argument paper**, circle **A**. Also, if the sentence presents an argument, underline the key words that indicate it is an argument thesis statement.

1. Over the past 15 years, companies have begun implementing many ways to make buildings more environmentally friendly.   R   A

2. Although the United States has instituted several policies that require factories to reduce emissions, the penalties for not meeting the policy standards must be more consistently applied in order to achieve positive results.   R   A

3. Those practicing modern medicine have recently begun exploring how more natural methods can be combined with technologically advanced treatments to achieve better outcomes.   R   A

4. The European Union (EU) has experienced its share of financial difficulties; however, it should not be abandoned.   R   A

5. The operating system of a PC computer is very different from that of an Apple computer.   R   A

6. Publicly traded companies need to institute more effective oversight policies, or those in charge will continue to make decisions that benefit them personally rather than the stockholders, even if it means committing illegal acts.   R   A

7. The completion of the railroad across the United States in the middle 1800s had far-reaching effects both socially and economically.   R   A

8. Bioinformatics, the analysis of biological information using math and computer science, is a field that we must continue to invest in if we want to find better treatment for diseases like cancer or diabetes.   R   A

9. Anthropologists define the word "tribe" in several different ways.   R   A

10. Emma Watson is one of the best actresses of the twenty-first century.   R   A

APA Style
[*Handbook*, Section 4J, pages 130–145]

. . . .
Exercise 4.6: APA Style Practice

Use the information provided for each publication to write a References entry in APA format.
Use the examples as models.

1. Book with 2 or more authors, edition other than first

Example:

> Aliber, R. Z., & Kindleberger, C.P. (2015). *Manias, panics, and crashes: A history of financial crises* (7th ed.). London: Palgrave Macmillan.

Date of publication: 2011

Title: Concise International and European IP Law

Edition: 2nd

Publisher: Kluwer Law International

Place of publication: London

Author: Thomas Cottier and Pierre Veron

_____

_____

2. Book by a group (corporate) author

Example:

> American Psychological Association. (2010). *Publication manual of the American Psychological Association* (6th ed.). Washington, DC: American Psychological Association.

Date of publication: 2007

Title: China: Five Thousand Years of History & Civilization

Publisher: City University of Hong Kong Press

Place of publication: Hong Kong

Author: The Editorial Committee of Chinese Civilization: A Source Book

_____

_____

3. Article or chapter in an edited volume

Example:

> O'Leary, A. O. (2017). Undocumented Mexican women in the U.S. justice system: Immigration, illegality and law enforcement. In C. Datchi & J. Ancis (Eds.), *Gender, psychology, and justice: The mental health of women and girls in the legal system* (pp. 254–279). New York, NY: New York University Press.

Date of publication: 2014

Book title: The Engagement of India: Strategies and Responses

Chapter title: India's Engagements with Southeast Asia: Singapore, Vietnam, and Indonesia

Page numbers: 147–168

Publisher: Georgetown University Press

Place of publication: Washington, DC

Editor: Ian Hall

Author: Donald Brewster

_____

_____

4. Journal article

Example:

> Hisschemöller, M. (2016). Cultivating the global garden. *Challenges in Sustainability, 4*(1), 28–38. doi: 10.12924/cis2016.04010028

Date of publication: June, 2017

Title of journal: International Political Science Review

Title of article: Does Exposure to Other Cultures Affect the Impact of Economic Globalization on Gender Equality?

Volume number: 38

Issue number: 3

Page numbers: 378–395

Authors: Pazit Ben-Nun Bloom, Sharon Gilad, Michael Freedman

Doi: 10.1177/0192512116644358

_____

_____

5. Article from online periodical

Example:

> Wild, S. (2017, 15 Mar.). Ghana telescope heralds first pan-African array. *Nature, 545.* Retrieved from http://www.nature.com.ezproxy.uvm.edu/news/ghana-telescope-heralds-first-pan-african-array-1.21958

Date of publication: April 22, 2015

Title of periodical: The Economist

Title of article: Recycling in America: In the Bin

Author: Edward Bartlett

URL: https://www.economist.com/democracyinamerica/2015/04/recycling-america

_____

_____

6. Online news article

Example:

> Alderton, B. (2017, May 5). Laguna council to consider extending citywide smoking ban. *LA Times.* Retrieved from http://www.latimes.com/socal/daily-pilot/tn-dpt-me-lb-council-preview-20170506-story.html

Date of publication: March 17, 2016

Title of news source: The Christian Science Monitor

Title of article: Did the Musical 'Hamilton' Save the Hamilton $10 bill?

Author: Olivia Lowenberg

URL: https://www.csmonitor.com/Business/2016/0317/Did-the-musical-Hamilton-save-the-Hamilton-10-bill-video

_____

_____

7. Non-periodical web document

Example:

> The United States Census Bureau. (2017). *U.S. population and world clock.* Retrieved from https://www.census.gov/popclock/

Date of publication: no date

Title of website: Cycling Advocacy Organizations

Author/Publisher: USA Cycling, Inc.

URL: https://www.usacycling.org/cycling-advocacy-organizations.htm

_____

_____

MLA Style
[*Handbook*, Section 4K, pages 146–165]

. . . .
Exercise 4.7: MLA Style Practice

Use the information provided for each publication to write a Works Cited entry in MLA format.
Use the examples as models.

1. Book with one author, edition other than first

Example:

   Steinbeck, John. *Of Mice and Men*. 4th ed., Penguin Books, 1993.

   Date of publication: 2017

   Author: Connor Goodpaster

   Publisher: Harvard Education Press

   Edition: 2nd

   Title: The Psyche of the American University Student

   _____

   _____

2. Book by a group (corporate) author

Example:

   Center for Chemical Process Safety. *Guidelines for Engineering Design for Process Safety*.
      2nd ed., Wiley-AIChE, 2013.

   Date of publication: 2017

   Author: National Oceanic and Atmospheric Association

   Publisher: U.S. Department of Commerce

   Edition: 3rd

   Title: Designing Education Projects to Encourage Students to Learn about the Weather

   _____

   _____

3. Work in an anthology, reference or collection / chapter in an edited volume

Example:

> Williams, Joseph M. "Defining Complexity." *Style in Rhetoric and Composition*, edited by Paul Butler, Bedford/St. Martin's, 2010, pp.186–201.

Date of publication: 2016

Author: Jill Cohen

Publisher: Ohio State University Press

Editor: Joan Wells

Title of book: Special Education: A Guide to Effective Public School Teaching

Title of article: How to Approach Standardized Testing

Page numbers: 45–53

_____

_____

4. Journal article with doi, obtained from a database

Example:

> Noel, Valerie A., et al. "Barriers to Employment for Transition-age Youth with Developmental and Psychiatric Disabilities." *Administration and Policy in Mental Health and Mental Health Services Research*, vol. 44, no. 3, 2017, pp. 354–358, *ProQuest Central*, doi:10.1007/s10488-016-0773-y.

Date of publication: 2013

Author: Kenneth R. Shelby, Thomas A. Mazzuchi, and Shahram Sarkani

Title of journal: Information Knowledge Systems Management

Title of article: Tacit Knowledge Mobilization Effect Due to Information Structure

Volume number: 12

Issue number: 2

Page numbers: 115–133

Database: Academic Search Elite

Doi: 10.3233/IKS-130220

_____

_____

5. Article from online periodical

Example:

> Eaton, Elizabeth. "Spray-On Mosquito Repellents Are More Effective Than Other Devices." *Science News,* 28 Mar. 2017, www.sciencenews.org/article/spray -mosquito-repellents-are-more-effective-other-devices?mode=magazine& context=193019.

Date of publication: July 21, 2017

Author: Julia Chang

Title of periodical: Forbes

Title of article: Your Career Choice Could Affect Your Marriage, According to This Study

URL: https://www.forbes.com/sites/learnvest/2017/07/21/your-career-choice-could-affect-your-marriage-according-to-this-study/#a05364f142f4

_____

_____

6. Online news article

Example:

> Pérez-Peña, Richard, and Sheryl Gay Stolberg. "Prosecutors Taking Tougher Stance in Fraternity Hazing Deaths." *New York Times,* 8 May 2017, www.nytimes.com/ 2017/05/08/us/penn-state-prosecutors-fraternity-hazing-deaths.html?ref= todayspaper&_r=0.

Date: July 23, 2017

Author: Avi Selk and Eva Ruth Moravic

Title of news source: The Washington Post

Title of article: 8 Were Found Dead Inside a Truck at a Texas Walmart – A 'Horrific' Case of Suspected Smuggling

URL: https://www.washingtonpost.com/news/post-nation/wp/2017/07/23/texas-tragedy-8-dead-including-children-found-locked-in-hot-truck-in-suspected-smuggling-case/?hpid=hp_hp-top-table-main_pn-texas-9am-retest%3Ahomepage %2Fstory&utm_term=.b3ff6022e992

_____

_____

7. Non-periodical web document, with author

Example:

> Fritz, Joanne. "Online Fundraising: A Startup Guide." *The Balance.* 16 Oct. 2016,
> 1:00pm, www.thebalance.com/online-fundraising-a-startup-guide-2502433.

Date: March 16, 2015

Author: Lee Rainie and Mary Madden

Website publisher: Pew Research Center

Section title: Americans' Views on Internet Surveillance Programs

URL: http://www.pewinternet.org/2015/03/16/americans-views-on-government-
surveillance-programs/

_____

_____

8. Online video

Example:

> "History Channel Documentary—Who Really Discovered America?—Documentary
> 2016." *YouTube*, uploaded by Discovery World, 25 Oct. 2016, www.youtube.com/
> watch?v=d_8aYdOPs3g.

Date: January 2015

Author: Roger Antonsen

Publisher: TED Talks

Title: Math is the Hidden Secret to Understanding the World

URL: https://www.ted.com/talks/roger_antonsen_math_is_the_hidden_secret_to_
understanding_the_world

_____

_____

GRAMMAR AND STYLE

- Word Form
- Articles
- Prepositions
- Word Choice in Formal Writing Style
- Reference Words
- Reducing Wordiness
- Subject-Verb Agreement
- Run-On Sentences and Sentence Fragments
- Comma Splice
- Adjective Clauses
- Parallel Structure
- Sentence Combining
- Sentence Variety

5

Word Form
[*Handbook,* Section 5A, pages 168–169]

. . . .
Exercise 5.1: Word Form Errors

Correct the word form error(s) in the sentences.

1. The lens acted as a prism, making the light looked like a rainbow.

2. Most of the mouse were used as control in the experiment.

3. The most common used material for computer keyboard is a type of polymer.

4. War are usually fought because a political power decides it wants more land.

5. The shipping of computer from the factory is usually done on Mondays and Wednesdays.

6. By law, families must use car seats for all child eight years old or younger.

7. After the invited speaker finished to talk, she took question from the audience.

8. It is important to be diplomat when dealing with a matter involving the development of

   a peace treaty among nations.

9. At the library you can find many different type of books.

10. Before write the paper, students should to make an outline.

Exercise 5.2: Word Forms

Fill in the blank with the correct word form. The base form of the needed word is provided.

1. After _____ [visit] his brother, he drove to Toronto.

2. Three _____ [woman] applied for the open position in the
   Sociology department.

3. In order to cook noodles, first you need _____ [boil] a pot of water.

4. The architect showed us several different _____ [design] for the
   entrance.

5. I was confused because the grocery store had been _____ [remodel]
   and the produce _____ [be] in a different location.

6. When we were standing next to it, the statue was _____ [surprising]
   tall.

7. They did not see any other _____ [bicycle] while they were riding on the
   trail.

8. Physics _____ [be] one of her favorite _____ [subject] in
   school.

9. The little girl sang _____ [beautiful] in the _____
   [crowd] auditorium.

10. You should _____ [research] carefully before _____
    [buy] a car.

Articles
[*Handbook*, Section 5B, pages 169–173]

. . . .
Exercise 5.3: Articles

In the paragraph, fill in the blanks with *a/an*, *the*, or 0 for zero article. Answers may vary in some contexts.

My hobby is oil painting. I often used to go to ① _____ museum to look at

② _____ various paintings. Among the artists, I preferred ③ _____ canvases of Maurice

Utrillo, ④ _____ French painter who mainly drew Montmartre in Paris. Utrillo had three

phases in his painting life: ⑤ _____ "montagny period," ⑥ _____ "colorist period," and ⑦

_____ "white period." I prefer ⑧ _____ paintings from the last phase. ⑨ _____ first paintings

he did are only like imitations of ⑩ _____ impressionists, and I cannot feel my favorite whitish

mood from his canvases. ⑪ _____ paintings from ⑫ _____ "colorist period" give us ⑬

_____ cheerful but too bright impression. On the other hand, Utrillo's paintings from ⑭

_____ "white period" move me deeply. ⑮ _____ whitish colors with ⑯ _____ various tones

make me feel melancholy. In addition, ⑰ _____ various tones of whites give me ⑱ _____

impressions of loneliness and isolation. I enjoy viewing ⑲ _____ Utrillo's paintings alone to

feel those moods and emotions that only he gives us through his "white period," and when

I paint ⑳ _____ pictures, I often imitate these tones because I wish to create ㉑ _____ similar

melancholy feeling.

Exercise 5.4: Articles

Underline the nouns in each sentence. Circle the article used or put 0 above the noun if there is no article. Then explain why *a/an*, *the*, or no article is used.

1. Hallway walls need to be painted every two or three years.

   Explanation:

   _____

   _____

2. The letter that I just received is from an old friend.

   Explanation:

   _____

   _____

3. I bought coffee from the Starbucks in the student union.

   Explanation:

   _____

   _____

4. You can often see Early American furniture in museums.

   Explanation:

   _____

   _____

5. Universities often have libraries with special collections.

   Explanation:

   _____

   _____

Exercise 5.5: Looking at Nouns in Context to Determine Article Use

Underline the nouns in the paragraph from a student essay. For each noun, notice whether *the*, *a/an*, or *zero article* is used with it. For each noun, give a reason for the type of article or zero article. [The sentences are numbered only for reference in this exercise.] Note: The meaning of a noun may also be limited or made more definite by using demonstratives (e.g., *those*), possessives (e.g., *my*), and quantifiers (e.g., *some*). In such cases, articles are not used.

① I remember one day when I was traveling to another city by train. ② The journey was very long. ③ Sitting next to me there was a family who had annoying and unbearable children. ④ It was a long and horrible day for me. ⑤ I had to bear the noise and misbehavior of the children. ⑥ I know that children make noise. ⑦ They go through a noisy phase that is part of life. ⑧ That's their job. ⑨ The children were only being children, doing what children do. ⑩ However, there is a limit to everything. ⑪ Those children went far beyond the limit. ⑫ As a passenger, I am entitled to have a peaceful and quiet environment when traveling. ⑬ These parents should have kept their children quiet. ⑭ Before taking a long trip, parents should teach their children how to behave in a public place or when using public transportation. ⑮ In this way, neither the passengers nor the parents would have a hard time on their trip, and everybody would be relaxed, especially me!

Exercise 5.6: Articles

In the paragraph, fill in the blanks with *a/an*, *the*, or 0 (for zero article). Be prepared to explain your answers. Answers may vary in some contexts.

Values and assumptions are different in each country. In _____ United States, high

levels of competition can affect _____ social relationships among youth and adults,

leading _____ people to consider themselves as single individuals who should

be ready to achieve their personal goals instead of being cooperative. Sometimes _____

competitiveness prevents young people from just enjoying their activities; they forget

that _____ primary purpose of _____ sports, music, and education is to enrich

our lives and to teach us how to live in our society. It is _____ problem because

_____ people are just focused on themselves. A major difference between _____

values of the United States and my country, Venezuela, is that we don't believe as much

as Americans in _____ competition. We believe more in cooperation with each

other. _____ example is that in America to find a job you need excellent skills and

abilities to stand out from the rest of _____ potential employees. However, in Venezuela

you just need to know people—the more contacts and more friends you have, the better.

That is _____ culture of finding _____ job in my country. Having _____ friend

or _____ family member is what is going to increase the chances of getting _____

employment. This shows how much we value _____ relationships in my country, but it

can be _____ drawback because Venezuelans are more prepared to be friendly than to

strive to be _____ best.

Prepositions
[*Handbook,* Section 5C, pages 174–175]

. . . .

Exercise 5.7: Prepositions

Insert the correct preposition in each gap in the paragraph. The first two have been done for you as examples.

I did hair cuts ① _for_ some friends recently, and I realized the process of hair-cutting is similar ② _to_ the writing process. When you start to cut hair for somebody, you need to figure ③ _____ the best style for this person, so you consult ④ _____ her or him, give some suggestions, and get some feedback. This is the same as generating ideas ⑤ _____ writing. Then you start cutting the hair ⑥ _____ the shape you designed. ⑦ _____ this stage, you don't work ⑧ _____ the details, but rather cut the hair ⑨ _____ each area such that you get a basic style. This phase compares ⑩ _____ drafting in writing. As you go on, you may find that the hairstyle you designed first is not good enough ⑪ _____ some ways. Therefore, you need to change it to fit the shape ⑫ _____ the person's face. Revising for writing is the same. Although this phase is similar for both hair-cutting and writing, there is a little difference ⑬ _____ them. In writing, you can delete some paragraphs and write new ones, but in hair-cutting you cannot put ⑭ _____ the hair that you have cut ⑮ _____. Last, when you are happy ⑯ _____ the shape and style of the haircut, you need to work ⑰ _____ some details, like the final editing stage in writing. You can smooth the edges ⑱ _____ the hair, or put some gel ⑲ _____ it, while in your essay you may want to check the spelling, punctuation, citations, or bibliography.

Exercise 5.8 Prepositions

Insert the correct preposition in each gap in the paragraph. Some blanks have more than one possible answer.

A Language of Wider Communication (LWC) is any language that allows communication

_____ speakers of different languages, either _____ a single country or

across national boundaries. In many countries, education is usually provided in the country's

LWC, and the national LWC is generally used _____ systems of government.

An LWC may be a language native to the region _____ which it is used (such as

Tok Pisin in Papua New Guinea), but this is not necessarily the case (as with English in

many countries). Sometimes a country uses an LWC that is a local or regional language,

not a major world language, which eases communication _____ citizens of that

country and enhances the sense of national identity. This is the case _____

Uzbekistan, for example, where the official language (and LWC) is Uzbek, which is not

widely spoken _____ of that country. Other countries may select the language

_____ former colonizers as the national LWC, as did many of the former French

colonies in Africa. This choice allows for easier communication _____ national

borders with other people who share the same LWC.

. . . .
Exercise 5.9 Phrasal Verbs

In each sentence a phrasal verb (verb plus one or more prepositions) is underlined. From the list of verbs, select one for each sentence to express a similar idea more formally. Use the correct form of the verb, and change any other grammar as necessary. The first one has been done for you as an example. One word is not used. Write your answers in the space provided.

analyze	cancel	~~confuse~~	continue
discard	discover	finish	fluctuate
improve	reduce	tolerate	

1. In his answer, Maurice <u>mixed up</u> two theories that should have been kept separate.

   In his answer, Maurice confused two theories that should have been kept separate.

2. Katherine can't <u>put up with</u> people who act in a superior manner.

3. We must carefully <u>break</u> this problem <u>down</u> into its components before we can find a solution.

4. When Anna <u>gets through with</u> the first project, she will immediately start the next one.

5. The dietician told me that I must <u>cut down on</u> my salt intake.

6. Octavia must <u>keep on</u> studying hard if she wants to pass the test

7. Professor Benatar <u>found out</u> why the volcano was emitting lava.

8. Leo <u>threw away</u> the damaged equipment.

9. The data indicate that the temperatures <u>go up and down</u> very much.

10. Due to bad weather, we had to <u>call off</u> our field trip to the science center.

Exercise 5.10: Phrasal Verbs

In the paragraph, replace the phrasal verbs with single-word verbs. Answers may vary.

There are several factors to <u>think about</u> when choosing a major or career. First, when a hobby <u>turns into</u> a profession it places a financial burden on that job that might make people less passionate about it. Moreover, sometimes people <u>find out</u> that something they love to do as a hobby does not provide enough income for them to be financially stable. Sometimes people who <u>bank on</u> their passion to be their sole source of income <u>end up</u> frustrated and exhausted when this <u>turns out</u> to be impossible. In effect, someone can feel fulfilled by their job even if it is not the primary thing that they love to do; instead, they can embrace their job and be satisfied by how well they can do the job. People will surely <u>come across</u> opportunities to pursue their passion outside of work. Students need to carefully consider these points when <u>picking out</u> a major and a future career. Then they can <u>figure out</u> what is really the best path for them.

Word Choice in Formal Writing Style
[*Handbook,* Section 5D, pages 176–177]

. . . .
Exercise 5.11: Word Choice

This short essay includes a variety of informal and general words, some of which have been underlined, and there may be additional words that you think are general and/or informal. Replace them with more formal or specific words above the underlined word(s). Be prepared to discuss your answers. Some word changes may require changing the sentence structure or adding a longer noun phrase. Answers may vary. [Paragraphs are numbered only for reference in this exercise.]

Away from Home

1. When I left my country and moved away from my family, I needed to learn new things. For example, I was awful at cooking before I came here, but now I am a good cook. Furthermore, I eat proper food and pay more attention to what I eat because if I get sick, nobody will take care of me. Although I do not have lots of time to spend on eating and cooking, I still insist on eating regularly and at home.

2. Another effect of leaving the family is having to manage everything better and without help. For instance, I have more time than before, and I can decide how to spend it. I do not need to get permission to do anything. I have made a study schedule for myself and have been following it day by day. It has already taken my parents lots of money to let me study here. Thus, I should manage my money well by not buying luxury things, comparing prices, and using coupons when I make purchases.

3. Finally, leaving my family and living by myself has been good for me because it made me grow up fast and get a sense of independence. It is very difficult for me to get used to this kind of life. Some things have changed and are different from before, such as my diet and my time and money management. However, I think I am getting an important and helpful lesson for my whole life. Such experiences are good for all people.

Reference Words
[*Handbook,* Section 5E, pages 178–181]

Exercise 5.12: Reference Words

Correct wrong or unclear references in each sentence, or insert synonyms in place of repetitive words or phrases. Answers may vary.

1. Professor Davis told Professor Lawson that his students were hard workers.

2. If the nations of the world all agreed to apply the same policies, they would be more successful.

3. Athletics at the Olympic level requires dedicated daily training. They actually spend years of their lives working towards this goal.

4. Several political campaigns were affected by unexpected global conflicts. The conflicts changed the way that voters viewed the candidates' positions.

5. Mary told me that there were two ways to interpret the experiment's results: one was that it was a well-conducted experiment and another was that its design was weak. I had not previously thought it was an issue.

6. The diplomats have refused to negotiate a ceasefire agreement, which is not acceptable.

7. The factory managers told the other employees that they would be getting an increase in their pay.

8. We emailed the office of the daily newspaper about the latest news, but it did not reply.

9. The typical romantic movie, it presents an unreal view of life.

10. Miguel said that I should be able to speak Spanish fluently because I lived there for a long time.

Reducing Wordiness
[*Handbook,* Section 5F, pages 181–183]

Exercise 5.13: Reducing Wordiness in Sentences

Revise the sentences to reduce wordiness. Write your answers in the space provided. Answers may vary.

1. His argument is not very persuasive because it is a weak argument that provides little evidence to show that it is valid.

2. After reading her report, we decided that the hiring policy regarding new workers should not be applied in our consideration of the hiring of anyone new.

3. If economists were to base their recommendations only on the data they receive from corporations, their recommendations would not be based on enough information to give good advice.

4. It is the opinion of Ms. MacDonald that we should not support any politicians who promise that everything will become perfect in the future if we vote for them.

5. From my viewpoint, study skills are very important skills that we can acquire that will help us when we are studying in school or college to advance our education.

Exercise 5.14: Reducing Wordiness in a Paragraph

Revise the paragraph to reduce wordiness. Write your answer in the space provided. Answers may vary.

These days there are many people exhibiting different types of behavior. Usually people's attitudes in a society and their behavior toward each other and society depend on the education and training they received from their parents when they were young, and that affects their future and their whole lives later on. Based on my own experience and people's habits in a society, it can be shown that parents influence their children's future. During my childhood, my parents taught me good values, the kind of attitudes that should be adopted socially and in every way, according to each situation of my life. In order to give me some proofs and examples, they also used to put into practice these values whenever it was necessary for them, and I grew up with those kinds of attitudes. They taught me honesty, integrity, and courtesy toward all.

Subject-Verb Agreement
[*Handbook*, Section 5H, pages 187–189]

. . . .

Exercise 5.15: Subject-Verb Agreement

If there is an error in the sentence, write **I** (for incorrect) in the blank, and correct the error. If there is no error, write **C** (for correct) in the blank.

_____ 1. Even though the answer are correct, the way in which you got the answer is not clear.

_____ 2. Each of the twelve questions have only one correct answer.

_____ 3. They decided to meet on Thursday to finish writing their programs, which are due on Friday.

_____ 4. In order to solve these problem, we need to first look at what is causing them.

_____ 5. Neither my teacher nor my advisor know the answer.

_____ 6. Many of the characters in the novel *The Lord of the Rings* are based on beings from Celtic mythology.

_____ 7. Both of the societies that we are studying in our textbook right now seems to share a common ideological foundation.

_____ 8. It has been proven that the majority of the population in each of those countries does not vote in the annual election.

_____ 9. It is difficult to determine whether the parent or the child were to blame.

_____ 10. The news these days are full of stories of violence.

Exercise 5.16: Subject-Verb Agreement

Write the suggested verb in the blank, making sure that it agrees with the subject.

Mastering a skill _____ [require] many hours of practice and hard

work. Some people _____ [suggest] that 10,000 hours of

practice _____ [is] necessary before truly becoming a master in

a particular skill. But is 10,000 hours a useful number, or is mastery more a matter

of natural talent and dedication? I believe that it's neither skill nor hard work. Very few

people _____ [reach] elite levels of athletic, musical, intellectual,

or artistic achievement. I do not believe that everyone who _____

[practice] a skill for more than 10,000 hours will become renowned for their skill. Someone

who _____ [work] hard for many years will certainly be highly skilled

in their field. But will they be a master? It is difficult to judge that. My brother, along with

several of his friends, _____ [have] been practicing judo for more than

ten years. They are all quite skilled and each of them _____ [have]

competed at the international level. There _____ [be] no doubt that

they have worked quite hard and have achieved a high level of skill in judo. Are they

masters in their sport? Have they reached the 10,000-hour mark? A better question may

be: Are they pursuing their passion and reaching their full potential while maintaining

physical and emotional health? This, rather than a mythical 10,000 hours of practice,

_____ [is] the best way to measure success.

Run-On Sentences and Sentence Fragments [*Handbook,* Section 5I, pages 190–192]

Exercise 5.17: Run-On Sentences and Fragments

Correct any run-on or fragment errors. Write your answers in the space provided. Answers may vary.

King Louis 14th demanded that the artists paint him as a god or mythological person and add more dignity to his portrait. The king in the paintings was thus painted wearing clothes of the emperors of ancient Rome and Greece. To send a message that he was the legitimate successor of the ancient empires. In these paintings, there were also goddesses and legendary heroes around the king to impress people with his honorable character. Moreover, the height of the king in paintings was always bigger than his real height all of the images were made to strengthen the authority of the king and government.

The famous palace of Versailles was designed to represent the authority and the power of the king in the clearest way. In this palace, many bureaucrats and noble families lived around the king, who was the center of the court the paintings or statues of him, as well as his symbols, were placed everywhere in the palace. People were surrounded by works of art. That were well planned to give a special impression. Therefore, it was difficult for citizens to be indifferent to the existence of the king at this palace.

Exercise 5.18: Fragments

Revise the sentences in the paragraph to correct the two sentence fragment errors.

In King Louis 14th's era, arts and new technologies were the most important ways of advertising. He and his court encouraged many kinds of arts and technology. To represent the power of the king. In the field of art, he established an organization of painters and patronized many artists including famous sculptors and architects. The Académie Française was established at this time. Since he wanted scholars to be studying the French language and to be cultivating it. In the field of science, we can say that the establishment of the national astronomical observatory was one of his main achievements.

Comma Splice
[*Handbook,* Section 5J, pages 193–194]

. . . .

Exercise 5.19: Comma Splices

Correct the comma splice errors in the paragraph. Answers may vary.

    Everyone needs smiles! You need a smile, for example, when you feel lonely or blue. When you are happy, it takes no effort to smile because it is already there. However, when you feel down, it is good to smile, how? It is easy. Lift your lips' edges. You do not need a big smile, just a little lift makes your mind lighter and warmer. I have to say that I do not know why this works, however, I have heard about a relationship between the physical and mental systems, they are interactive, when you are happy, a smile appears on your face. When you make a smiling face, you can make yourself feel happy. After I heard about this, I tried it, it worked!

Adjective Clauses [*Handbook,* Section 5K, pages 195–197]

Exercise 5.20: Comma Use in Adjective Clauses

Correct the errors in adjective clauses in the paragraph.

The liver is the most important organ that is affected by alcohol. The liver which is the largest organ in the body removes or detoxifies poisons, germs, and bacteria from the blood, makes protein, and produces immune agents. Although direct damage from alcohol in the liver cells has not been reported, alcohol and its metabolites injure the liver by blocking its normal metabolism of proteins, fats, and carbohydrates. As a consequence, consuming alcohol on a regular basis causes fatty liver, alcoholic hepatitis, and alcoholic liver cirrhosis which all prevent the normal functioning of the body. For example, blood may accumulate in the leg and in the abdomen. In addition, bleeding, that cannot be stopped easily, develops when the protein-making function of the liver is destroyed. Gallstones, itching, and jaundice which is the yellowing of the skin and eyes also result because of deteriorating bile metabolism. If the liver is not able to detoxify poisons from the blood, these toxins accumulate in the blood and finally in the brain. People, who have these problems, are likely to suffer from personality changes, mental symptoms, coma, and even death.

Parallel Structure
[*Handbook,* Section 5L, pages 198–199]

Exercise 5.21: Parallel Structure

Find and correct errors in parallelism in the paragraph. Answers may vary.

Governments frequently divert what science produces into war-related uses. The original reason for scientists inventing things is usually to improve technology and helping people live better. For example, the purpose of inventing the airplane was to shorten travel time, and dynamite was invented for people to remove mountains and they could build houses there more easily. However, governments changed the purpose of those technologies. The airplane has been changed into a military equipment transporter or carrying bombs, and they made dynamite into a killing tool in these bombs. It is true that people spend a lot of money on researching new technology for a better life; however, a lot more money is spent for development of the new technology into new weapons.

Sentence Combining
[*Handbook,* Section 5M, pages 200–204]

· ·
Exercise 5.22: Combining Sentences

Combine the pairs or groups of simple sentences. Try to change the meanings as little as possible. Answers may vary.

1. Memory is a vital quality of human thought. Without memory we would not be able to function in our daily activity.

2. Memory failures do happen frequently. This causes many problems, such as forgetting important information that we studied for an exam.

3. When studying for an exam, you can use different techniques to improve how much you remember the important points. You can highlight the points in your textbook with a marker pen. You can write a summary of the important points on file cards. You can recite the important points out loud to yourself.

4. I make up possible exam questions based on my class notes. It's a study method I learned from my aunt. She was a professor of psychology. This method has always been the most effective one for me.

5. Study your class notes before a test. Put the notes aside. Then say the main points out loud, as if you are telling someone what they are. It will help you remember them.

6. I learned a valuable study method from my friend. My friend William seems to remember his class notes very well. It helped me a lot.

7. William advised me not to leave my studying until just before a test. He said that I should have shorter study sessions of the same material every day. He had found this approach to be much more effective than trying to remember everything in one long study session.

8. Memory is affected by repetition. Highlight the important points in your textbook. Read them again and again over a period of several days.

9. Some students use mnemonics to help them remember facts. A mnemonic is a memory aid. A mnemonic can be a made-up word, a verse, or other verbal or visual device.

10. I found it hard to remember the colors of the rainbow. Then I learned a simple mnemonic that sounds like a person's name. The mnemonic is "Roy G. Biv." It uses the first letter of each color: red, orange, yellow, green, blue, indigo, violet.

Exercise 5.23: Using Specific Structures to Revise Sentences

Rewrite the sentences using the suggested structure. Combine sentences when necessary.
Answers may vary.

1. I was very unwilling to take the course in trigonometry. I took the course. **[adverb]**

2. During the 1980s Tim Berners-Lee developed the foundation of what we now call the Web with his work on information retrieval from distributed systems. **[passive]**

3. We missed our flight due to Stanley's failure to arrive on time. **[divided sentence]**

4. Janet had studied hard for the final examination in her Biology class. She was sure that she would do very well on it. **[dependent clause]**

5. Paulina was encouraged by her good results on the final History exam. She thought that she might take a more advanced course in the next semester. **[participial phrase]**

6. Alexander Fleming discovered penicillin when he observed that mold would not grow around a bacteria culture that he had unintentionally left uncovered. **[passive]**

7. Alfonso traveled to Ecuador, where his family was still living. He was happy to go there. **[adverb]**

8. I did not say "basketball." I said Enrico is very skilled at tennis. **[divided sentence]**

9. I wished that I had studied harder for the spelling test. I arrived at school in a state of anxiety. **[participial phrase]**

10. It was not easy to develop a new research program to better understand how the sun transmits radiation. Professor Bigelow and her graduate students were successful in their work and published an article about it. **[dependent clause]**

Sentence Variety
[*Handbook,* Section 5N, pages 205–208]

Exercise 5.24: Creating More Variety in Sentence Structure

Rewrite the paragraph so that there is more variety in the sentence structure. Write your answer in the space provided. Answers may vary.

The use of fossil fuels has increased greatly. Coal, natural gas, and oil are fossil fuels. Fossil fuels are becoming hard to find. Using more ethanol would be better than relying too much on fossil fuels. Ethanol has advantages that are clear. Ethanol's big advantage is that it can be made from many common crops. Sugar cane, corn, and wheat are examples of possible sources of ethanol. Growing more of these crops can help farmers increase their income. However, these crops are also needed as food for humans and livestock. A choice has to be made sometimes between growing crops for food and growing crops for fuel. It's a difficult choice. Reducing the supply of food crops causes an immediate increase in food prices. Many of the world's people are hungry and need these crops as food. However, with cheaper fuel, farmers can grow crops more efficiently. They use fuel-powered equipment for planting and reaping crops. This can increase their production of crops.

SECTION 6

PUNCTUATION

- Period
- Question Mark
- Exclamation Point
- Comma
- Semicolon
- Colon

6

Period
[*Handbook*, Section 6A, pages 210–211]

Exercise 6.1: Period at End of Sentence: Run On

Each sentence has a punctuation error that has resulted in a run-on sentence. Correct the error by inserting a period in the appropriate position. Correct capitalization as necessary.

1. Machines can be helpful if you understand them some people don't like any machines.

2. When the sun is shining, I go swimming when it rains, I go swimming too because I love swimming.

3. Monarch butterflies have a very distinctive look they are a beautiful orange color with black and white markings.

4. I would very much like to travel to foreign countries as soon as possible which ones I will go to will not be certain until I determine the costs of air travel.

5. The raw material of statistics is data or numbers the data are the result of counting or measurement that assigns numbers to objects.

6. Biostatistics focuses only on biological and medical science areas there are many biostatistics applications in clinical data.

7. Descriptive statistics is organizing and summarizing data to determine what information the data contain to organize and summarize data, we can use methods such as order array or measuring the central tendency by mean, median, and mode for population or grouped data.

8. Diabetes can be divided into two categories one is Insulin Dependent Diabetes and the other is Non-Insulin Dependent Diabetes.

9. It is important to drink enough water to avoid dehydration many people do not drink enough water doctors recommend 8 glasses a day.

10. There are many problems in the field of global education basically they arise from the fact that so many children do not attend primary school, so more advanced education is not possible.

Exercise 6.2: Period at End of Sentence: Correcting Errors

In the paragraph, the wrong punctuation has been inserted where the periods should be. Make the necessary corrections.

1. She looked out to sea, to her left were some ships? Far beyond the ships, she saw some whales and dolphins, she saw only cliffs and crashing waves to her right, she decided then that she would try to find a ship that would accept her as a passenger for the long journey across the ocean? She was determined to cross the Pacific and begin her search—

2. He didn't know where he had left his keys? He looked all over the house for them, he couldn't seem to find them in any of the usual places. He had to go to work he would be late! He realized that maybe they were in an unusual place? He looked under the cushions of the living room sofa and he looked under the refrigerator, he spent more than an hour looking for them, finally he found them in the bathtub . . .

Exercise 6.3: Period with Decimals

Use numerals with periods in the correct places to express each amount.

1. three and four hundredths _____

2. sixty-four thousand dollars and no cents _____

3. one and six hundredths _____

4. seven and eighty-six hundredths_____

5. two million dollars and two cents _____

6. fourteen and fourteen hundredths _____

7. nine and nine tenths _____

8. one hundred thirty-two dollars and seventy-five cents _____

Question Mark
[*Handbook*, Section 6B, page 212]

Exercise 6.4: Question Mark and Period

Some of the sentences in the paragraph are questions, and some are not. Place periods or question marks in the appropriate places. Capitalize as necessary. Remember that a question mark is not placed after indirect (reported) questions.

The detective sat in his office thinking about the strange events at the time of the crime These were his thoughts: Who was the second witness why had she vanished so quickly there were many people who wanted to know he knew that Anne wanted to know Sally had asked questions about it Andrew had also made inquiries James, however, had asked only two questions he had asked when the crime occurred he had also asked why it had been committed that was very strange why had James not asked about the second witness Did he perhaps know where she was it would probably be a good idea to question James about his movements after the crime

Exclamation Point
[*Handbook*, Section 6C, page 213]

. . . .

Exercise 6.5: Exclamation Point for Strong Feeling

Decide which of the following sentences or phrases express strong feeling, and place exclamation points after them. In other cases, use a period or question mark.

1. Oh, no

2. Did you find the new location easily

3. The painting was rather unusual, with a turtle shown in a strange mixture of green, blue, pink, and various shades of red

4. How strange

5. Who is that man carrying the book

6. I can't believe I forgot

7. Are you able to come to the meeting

8. What an amazing opportunity

Exercise 6.6: Exclamation Points, Periods, or Question Marks in a Conversation

Place exclamation points, periods, or question marks in the appropriate places in the dialogue.

Customer: How much is this pair of shoes

Clerk: Ninety-nine dollars

Customer: That's so expensive

Clerk: Not really, considering what they are made of

Customer: What are they made of

Clerk: A special, rare material originally designed for astronauts' boots for use in outer space

Customer: How amazing perhaps I'll buy a pair

Comma
[*Handbook*, Section 6D, pages 214–223]

Exercise 6.7: Comma after Introductory or Transitional Words and Phrases

Place commas, if needed, after the introductory words and phrases in the sentences.

1. It is customary to place a comma after introductory or transitional words and phrases.

2. Remembering all the serious obstacles faced the previous year Janet refused to try again.

3. Having gone over the material carefully in study group Dominique felt ready for the test.

4. As a means of repairing torn cloth nothing could be better than this special machine.

5. Being a lazy student from my earliest schooldays I naturally found it hard to pass examinations.

6. Natalie had become fluent and had made many new friends during her semester abroad.

7. After speaking to his bank manager the wheat farmer was able to get a loan to enable him to continue farming for another year.

8. At the restaurant Ivan and Olga met many journalists whom they had not seen for fifteen years.

9. The letters that were addressed to me were finally delivered to the right address.

10. Except for the writing class my studies at the Language Institute are very easy.

11. After understanding English comma usage the students will find all the other marks of punctuation relatively easy.

12. Moreover it was absolutely impossible for the ambassador to visit the Prime Minister.

Exercise 6.8: Comma after Introductory Clauses

Place commas, if needed, after the introductory clauses in the sentences.

1. When winter comes I will go skiing.

2. He will buy a bag of oranges if he goes to the supermarket.

3. After Leo's cousin arrives in Tasmania they will travel together to the north of the island.

4. Very many students agree that the university offers excellent courses.

5. Unless they can travel to an English-speaking country students must learn the language in their own countries.

6. Students who want to learn English travel to English-speaking countries if they can.

7. Because certain unusual events have occurred the detectives are investigating the case.

8. Many people do not smoke because it would affect their health.

9. If my phone is broken I will need to replace it right away.

10. Since it rained all day we were not able to go to the park.

Exercise 6.9: Comma before Coordinating Conjunctions Linking Independent Clauses

Place commas, if needed, before the coordinating conjunctions in the sentences. When both clauses are very short (about five words or less), the commas can be left out to emphasize a strong connection between the clauses.

1. There has been an increase in the popularity of volleyball and many more spectators are attending the games.

2. Some of the tennis players were doing special exercises to improve their game but others were just relaxing in the clubhouse.

3. The women from that country did not like golf nor did they like cricket.

4. Igor will travel to Uruguay to start a new branch of his business or he will stay in his country for two more years and then go to Uruguay.

5. My chemistry teacher keeps very busy since he also does a lot of research.

6. They left the house on time but they were late to the theater because of an accident.

7. Jane gave me advice and I succeeded.

8. As it was the only drink available at the small cafeteria we drank many cups of strong coffee.

9. The research teams in the computer industry always try to find out what the competition is working on and they then try to bring out similar or better products.

10. To make a good pizza at home you should have the right ingredients and prepare them in the right way.

Exercise 6.10: Comma with Lists of Words, Phrases, or Clauses

If the sentences include a list of three or more words, phrases, or clauses, separate the items from each other by placing a comma after each item in the list.

1. Books papers bottles cans pens and pencils were lying scattered on the floor of the room.

2. Jennifer decided to study economic theory business administration personnel management and computer programming.

3. Jennifer's sister could not decide whether to study art French or linguistics.

4. James refused to go to the store because it was raining very hard because he felt tired and because there was enough food in the house.

5. If a politician smiles at you promises you something wonderful claims to have done many good things or criticizes his opponents you can guess that there must be an election soon.

6. Financial advice loans and credit cards were all offered by the new bank.

7. The travel advertisement promised an ideal holiday in South America, with visits to Brazil Paraguay Argentina and Chile.

8. The journalist said that all countries need to diversify their energy sources find more fossil fuels and conserve fuel supplies in order to ensure that energy resources are adequate.

9. The complaints to the mayor mentioned problems with parking facilities traffic flow public transportation unsafe pedestrian crossings and special paths for bicycles.

10. Swimming walking jogging and dance are all good forms of exercise for busy students.

Exercise 6.11: Comma with Coordinate Adjectives

Separate coordinate adjectives from each other by placing a comma between them. Do not place a comma between the last adjective and the noun. Do not separate cumulative adjectives. (Adjectives that can be joined by *and* are coordinate; adjectives that cannot be joined by *and* are cumulative and are not separated by commas.)

1. Senator Pulinski is a tough outspoken critic of the President's foreign policy.

2. A big fluffy gray cat is always coming into our yard.

3. It was a difficult bumpy long twisting road that led to the farmhouse on the side of the mountain.

4. The student said that her history class was always interesting very informative and quite stimulating.

5. Due to a severe system-wide problem with spam and viruses, our company installed a complicated computer protection program on all our machines.

6. Our walk in the woods turned out to be cold wet and tiresome instead of the pleasant relaxing stroll that we had expected.

7. The best exhibit in the art gallery was a ten-foot-wide concrete and metal statue of a horse and rider.

8. The Queen's chefs prepared a delicious mildly-spicy special dish for her fifteen dinner guests.

9. Even though she was tired, the loud buzzing noise kept her awake.

10. The Himalayas, where Mount Everest is located, are a huge awe-inspiring mountain range in Asia.

Exercise 6.12: Comma with Quotations

Place commas before and after the direct quotations (the words actually spoken). Leave out the comma when a quotation begins or ends a sentence and when the quotation ends with a question mark or exclamation point.

1. Yoo-Jin wrote "These two advertisements can be compared in several aspects."

2. "The women's salaries are higher than the average salary of men in that business" asserted Nina.

3. "Excuse me," the customer asked "where can I find the reference section?"

4. Sachiko exclaimed "But that was my idea!"

5. "This design will appeal to young, fashionable people. We must use it in our next product" said the artist to the manager.

6. "I prefer" said Hannah, pointing at the book "to stay at home alone to read this. It's so interesting! It's about English grammar."

7. "The style and purpose of this musical composition are fascinating" said Jessie.

8. "Online purchases were more than half of the sales in the first quarter, signifying a major new direction for the company" according to a report released by Frew and Macmillan Corporation.

9. A professor of business studies wrote "In electronic transactions, transparency of price, design, availability, and supplier produces more choices and better pricing."

10. "Industrial development near the city is the key to our progress" announced the mayor.

Exercise 6.13: Comma with Abbreviations

Place commas, as needed, in the sentences.

1. This course for first-year students helps with many things e.g. study skills time management etc.

2. The important issue in this election is tax credits for individual citizens i.e. indirectly returning some funds to them.

3. During the test you must remove all bags, books, papers etc. from the desk.

4. Smith et al. wrote the book about prehistoric times that I studied in my anthropology course.

5. Abbreviations should be limited to situations where they help the reader i.e. when comprehension would be increased by using them.

6. Take some extra food, clothing etc. on this trip because it may take longer than planned.

7. I do not support the program promoted by Mr. Ross et al.

8. Several new books have been published recently on this topic e.g. *The Brain's Way of Healing*.

Exercise 6.14: Comma with Contrasting or Interrupting Elements or Those Needing Separation for Clarity

Place a comma, if needed, before and after contrasting or interrupting elements or those needing separation for clarity. Omit the first comma if the interrupting element begins the sentence. Omit the second comma if the interrupting element ends the sentence.

1. Amelia's husband by contrast is a strict vegetarian.

2. This computer though excellent is not the type they need.

3. Therefore the square of the hypotenuse is equal to the sum of the squares of the other two sides.

4. Would you like to sing now Ms. Johnson?

5. Our shoes are you know the best available even if they are the most expensive.

6. Students who want to attend college must be very diligent.

7. Sounding quite excited she spoke about her trip to New Zealand.

8. I accepted the suggestion of painting the walls red and orange because the room needed brightening.

9. Will you please be as quiet as possible during the recording?

10. Secondly place the apples in a dish with the other fruit.

11. My flute which I got for my 12th birthday is one of my most prized possessions.

12. Our reading teacher bought a fine car from the second hand car dealer on Forbes Avenue.

13. We arrived in this great city in September of 1977.

14. Angela despite her injured foot won the long jump.

15. This book not the one that is on the table is his.

16. I think that given no serious or unexpected obstacles we will complete our research project before the middle of March.

Semicolon
[*Handbook*, Section 6E, pages 224–225]

Exercise 6.15: Semicolon with Independent Clauses

Use semicolons to separate independent clauses, coordinate clauses, or items in a list. (Note that the semicolons are made necessary by the internal punctuation of clauses or listed items.)

1. All flights in and out of the airport have been canceled the storm is predicted to hit early this afternoon.

2. Do not go back to the beginning if you make a mistake just keep going until you finish the job.

3. There was a variety of objects lying on the floor: old books, most of them with torn covers sheets of paper, thrown down by the clerks empty containers, which had obviously been used for paint and many empty shoeboxes.

4. After the party we returned to school, driving along the old highway, a dangerous road, luckily for us, we made it back safely.

5. In order to use the machine you should first remove the dust cover then press the green button, which starts the motor going then turn the speed control, at the top left, to the desired speed and, finally, adjust the heat control to the desired temperature.

6. The traveling circus transported many things, including large tents animals, safely secured in cages musical instruments of all types and costumes that were specially designed for each performer.

7. The film, which was very interesting, helped us to understand the special uses of magnetism, electricity, and heat and the presentation, as usual at such conferences, was followed by a general discussion.

Exercise 6.16: Semicolon

Necessary semicolons have been left out of the sentences. Insert them in the appropriate places.

1. On the cover of the catalog there were pictures of an electronic clock, selling for only $10 a steam iron, which cost $22.99 a gift-wrapped box, with no indication of what was inside it and a camera, complete with flash and leather carrying case.

2. A lot of money is spent on preserving our nation's water supply, which involves taking care of rivers, lakes, dams, and reservoirs but it remains a difficult task.

3. Everything went wrong yesterday: the children, who were late for school, started fighting my car, bought just a month earlier, would not start my best friend, recently recovered from a serious illness, called to say he was feeling sick again and my boss, a pleasant, kind man, told me that I might lose my job.

4. The photocopier seemed to be failing: the paper kept getting jammed there were large dark streaks in the middle of all the photocopies and the machine gave an error message when it was turned on.

5. The first problem is that, in order to pay college fees, students must get loans, grants, or scholarships and the second problem is that they must study hard to pass the difficult exams.

Colon [*Handbook*, Section 6F, pages 226–228]

. . . .

Exercise 6.17: Colon

Place colons in the appropriate places in the sentences.

1. They purchased many things after winning the lottery two new cars, a vacation home and a boat.

2. She read two long novels over her winter break *Anna Karenina* and *The Tale of Genji*.

3. Our class meets on Tuesdays at 9 45, not 8 45.

4. In the introduction to his famous book, *The Origin of the Species*, Charles Darwin begins

   When on board H.M.S. "Beagle," as a naturalist, I was much struck with certain facts in the distribution of the organic beings inhabiting South America, and in the geological relations of the present to the past inhabitants of that continent. These facts, as will be seen in the latter chapters of this volume, seemed to throw some light on the origin of the species—that mystery of mysteries, as it has been called by one of our greatest philosophers.

5. The young boy had the following in his pockets string, used chewing gum, pebbles, a catapult, some pennies, twigs, a broken pencil, and a few marbles.

6. The Japanese poet Basho once said "Do not seek to follow in the footsteps of the wise; seek what they sought."

7. Professor Jones began to write the recommendation letter for her best student, which began,

   To the Admissions Committee

   I am writing in support of Clara Morgan's application to your PhD program in Civil Engineering.

8. For this recipe, use a ratio of 31 (three to one)—three parts water and one part rice.

9. The odds against my horse winning are 52 (five to two).

10. As Ismael cleaned his room, he found the following items under the bed a dirty sock, two of his favorite comic books, and the homework assignment he could not find the night before.

11. To his surprise, Guiseppe found three English proverbs that referred to Rome "All roads lead to Rome," "Rome was not built in a day," and "When in Rome, do as the Romans do."

12. Leilani's daily work schedule is as follows check for mail, reply to urgent letters, attend meetings, have a business lunch, work with the planning department, and finally attend to mail orders.